Hospital Jokes

Hospital jokes

Dilwyn Phillips

© Dilwyn Phillips & Y Lolfa 2009

This book is subject to copyright and may not be reproduced by any means except for review purposes without the prior, written consent of the publishers.

ISBN: 978-1-84771-103-8

Cartoons by Morgan Tomos

Printed on acid-free and partly recycled paper
and published and bound in Wales by
Y Lolfa Cyf., Talybont, Ceredigion SY24 5HE
e-mail ylolfa@ylolfa.com
website www.ylolfa.com
tel (01970) 832 304
fax 832 782

Contents

Introduction

Members of the medical profession have to have a good sense of humour. It is said humour promotes health and wellbeing by stimulating a playful discovery, expression or appreciation of the absurdity of life's situations.

Humour is a social tool that is often used to ease and diffuse tense and difficult situations. By laughing at problems a person can ease stress and other painful emotions. For example, when a person or group of people need to perform difficult or disturbing tasks, like dealing with trauma or death, everyone knows that the occasional irreverent comment can sometimes diffuse the tension and keep the horror at bay.

Black humour is a way of keeping a mental distance between oneself and what one is doing, and it will always be ever-present. It is not actually meant to be derogatory or disrespectful: even though it may sound so to others in that moment, it is merely a way for any person to deal with a difficult situation.

Black humour should be contrasted with sick humour. In sick humour, much of the humorous element comes from shock and revulsion. In black humour it usually includes an element of irony, or even fatalism. A good example of black humour is a man taking off his belt to hang himself, and his trousers falling down.

Unpredictable bursts of laughter, like lightning, relieve the tension and clear the atmosphere.

Did you know that laughter can reduce stress, boost your immune system, help reduce your blood pressure, and exercise certain muscles (diaphragm, abdominal, facial, neck, back, and leg).

Looking for a quick easy way to 'work out'? Laugh! Did you know that laughing 100 times is the equivalent to 15 minutes on an exercise bike or 10 minutes on a rowing machine? Amazing, isn't it?

As I am married to a retired nurse, I have overheard anecdotes, stories and observations and some really funny happenings, some perfectly true stories, and others... well, see what you think!

Just enjoy it!

Dilwyn Phillips

General Practitioners

Tom and Megan were playing on the ninth green when Megan collapsed from a heart attack.

"Please dear, I need help," she said.

Tom ran off saying, "I'll go get some help." Some time later he returned, picked up his club and began to line up his shot on the green. Megan, on the ground, raised up her head and said, "I'm dying and you're putting?"

"Don't worry, dear. I found a doctor on the second hole who said he'd come and help you."

"The second hole? When the hell is he coming?"

"Hey! I told you not to worry." Tom said, practicing his putt. "Everyone's already agreed to let him play through."

* * *

A car skidded on a wet pavement and struck a telephone pole. Several onlookers ran over to help the driver.

A woman was the first to reach the victim, but Nigel rushed in and pushed her aside. "Step aside, lady," he said. "I've taken a course in first-aid!" The woman watched for a few minutes, then tapped Nigel on the shoulder.

"Pardon me," she said. "But when you get to the part about calling a doctor, I'm right here."

* * *

A couple are out walking in the hills when one of them falls to the ground. He doesn't seem to be breathing and his eyes are rolled back in his head. Andy whips out his mobile phone and calls 999. He gasps to the operator, "My friend Will is dead! What can I do?"

The operator, in a calm soothing voice says, "Just take it easy, I can help. First, we have to ascertain that he is dead."

There is a silence, then a shot is heard. Andy's voice comes back on the line. He says, "OK, now what?"

* * *

Megan went to her doctor's surgery. She was seen by one of the new doctors, but after about four minutes in the examination room, she burst out screaming and ran down the hall.

An older doctor stopped her and asked what the problem was, so she explained. He had her sit down and relax in another room.

The older doctor marched back to the first and demanded, "Dr Griffiths, what's the matter with you? Megan Jones is 63 years-old, she has four grown children and seven grandchildren, and you told her she was pregnant?"

Dr Griffiths smiled smugly as he continued to write on his clipboard.

"Cured her hiccups though, didn't it?"

* * *

Beth, now in her thirties, is at home happily jumping unclothed on her bed and squealing with delight.

Her husband Rob watches her for a while and asks, "Do you have any idea how ridiculous you look? What's the matter with you?"

Beth continues to bounce on the bed and says, "I don't care what you think. I just came from having a mammogram and the doctor says that not only am I healthy, but I have the breasts of an 18-year-old."

Rob replies, "What did he say about your 42-year-old arse?"

"Your name never came up," she said.

* * *

"How are you feeling today, Mrs Thomas?" asked the doctor.

"I'm not really feeling myself today, doctor," she replied.

"Oh, I am glad of that," said the doctor, "that was a nasty habit you had!"

* * *

Susan complained to her friend Jane that love-making with her husband was becoming routine and boring.

"Get creative, Susan. Break up the monotony. Why don't you try 'playing doctor' for an hour? That's what I do," said Jane.

"Sounds great," Susan replied, "but how do you make it last for an hour?"

"That's easy… just keep him in the waiting room for 59 minutes!"

* * *

Rob had been away serving with the army in Bosnia. When he came home he discovered that his wife was eight months pregnant. This worried Rob, as he'd been away for almost eleven months. So he went to have a talk with his doctor.

Dr Jones explained to Rob that this was quite possible, by explaining that it was called a grudge pregnancy.

"What sort of pregnancy is that?" enquired Rob.

"Oh," replied the doctor, "it means that someone had it in for you!"

* * *

Sandra was prescribed some suppositories by her doctor. A few weeks later, she revisited him and he asked her how they had worked.

"Doctor," said Sandra, "for all the use they were, I may as well have shoved them up my arse!"

* * *

John walked into a crowded doctors' surgery. As he approached the desk, the receptionist asked, "Yes sir, may we help you?"

"There's something wrong with my dick," John replied.

The receptionist became aggravated and said, "You shouldn't come into a crowded office and say things like that."

"Why not? You asked me what was wrong and I told you," said John.

"We do not use language like that here," she said. "Please go outside and come back in and say that there's something wrong with your ear or whatever."

John shrugged his shoulders, walked out, waited several minutes and re-entered. The receptionist smiled smugly and asked, "Yes?"

"There's something wrong with my ear," he stated. The receptionist nodded approvingly. "And what is wrong with your ear, sir?"

"I can't piss out of it," John replied.

* * *

Having finished examining Simon, the doctor said, "I can't find a cause for your complaint. Frankly, I think it's due to drinking."

"In that case," said Simon, "I'll come back when you're sober."

* * *

One day, after Alec had his annual medical, the doctor came out and said, "You had a great check-up. Is there anything that you'd like to talk about or ask me?"

"Well," he said, "I was thinking about getting a vasectomy."

"That's a pretty big decision. Have you talked it over with your family?"

"Yeah, and they're in favour 15 to 2."

* * *

A man with a glass eye had been out for a night on the town. Being the worse for wear, he stumbled into bed and dropped his glass eye into his drinking water on the bedside table. During the night, he drank the water and swallowed the eye.

A day or so later he was suffering from severe constipation, so he went to his GP. The doctor inserted his proctoscope and muttered under his breath, "Good grief, I've looked up plenty of arseholes before, but this is the first one to ever look back at me!"

* * *

Anne goes to the doctor complaining of her constant flatulance. She says, "Doctor, I must fart 500 times a day, but you would never know it, because they're silent and they don't smell. For instance, I've just passed gas at least 20 times just sitting here with you right now."

The doctor just nods and gives her a prescription. He tells her to come back in two weeks.

Two weeks later Anne enters his office and says, "Those pills made my farting worse! I'm still breaking wind 500 times day, but now they smell really bad!"

The doctor replies, "Well, now that we've cleared up your sinuses, we can work on your hearing!"

* * *

Wendy, an elderly woman, went into the doctors' surgery. When the doctor asked why she was there, she replied, "I'd like to have some birth control pills."

Taken aback, the doctor thought for a minute and then said, "Excuse me, Mrs Jones, but you're 72 years old. What possible use could you have for birth control pills?"

Wendy responded, "They help me sleep better."

The doctor thought some more and continued, "How in the world do birth control pills help you to sleep?"

Wendy said, "I put them in my granddaughter's orange juice every morning and I sleep better at night."

* * *

80-year-old Norman was having his annual check-up and the doctor asked him how he was feeling.

"I've never been better!" Norman boasted. "I've got an 18-year-old bride who's pregnant and having my child! What do you think about that?"

The doctor considered this for a moment, then said, "Let me tell you a story, Norman. I knew a guy who was a keen hunter. He never missed a season. But one day, he went out in a bit of a hurry, and he accidentally grabbed his umbrella instead of his gun. So he was in the woods," the doctor continued, "and suddenly a grizzly bear appeared in front of him. He raised up his umbrella, pointed it at the bear and squeezed the handle. And do you know what happened?"

"No," replied Norman, dumbfounded.

"The bear dropped dead in front of him!"

"That's impossible!" exclaimed Norman. "Someone else must have shot the bear."

"That's kind of what I'm getting at," replied the doctor.

* * *

Gareth hasn't been feeling well, so he goes to his doctor for a complete check-up.

Afterwards the doctor comes out with the results.

"I'm afraid I have some very bad news," the doctor says. "You're dying, and you don't have much time left."

"Oh, that's terrible!" says Gareth. "How long have I got?"

"Ten," the doctor says sadly.

"Ten?" Gareth asks. "Ten what? Months? Weeks? What?"

"Nine... eight... seven..."

* * *

"Doc, I can't stop singing 'The Green, Green Grass of Home'."

"That sounds like Tom Jones Syndrome."

"Is it common?"

"It's not unusual."

* * *

Dr Jones decided that he wanted to return to China to see the Great Wall for a second time, so he called the Chinese Embassy and asked about the documents he needed. After a lengthy discussion about passports, he was reminded that he needed a visa.

"Oh no I don't, I've been to China many times and never had to have one of those." The office double-checked and sure enough, his stay required a visa.

He responded, "Look, I've been to China four times and every time they have accepted my American Express."

* * *

Paddy goes to the doctor with problems to his posterior.

"Doctor, it's me ahrse. I'd like you to have a look, if you would."

So the doctor gets him to drop his pants and takes a look. "Incredible," he says, "there is a £20 note lodged up here." Tentatively he eases the note out of the Paddy's bottom, and another £10 pound note appears.

"This is amazing!" exclaims the doctor. "What do you want me to do?"

"Well for goodness' sake take it out, man!" shrieks Paddy.

The doctor pulls out the tenner and another twenty appears, and another, and another, and another. Finally the last note comes out and no more appear.

"Ah doctor, thank you very much indeed, that's much better. Just out of interest, how much was in there then?"

The doctor counts the pile of cash and says "£1,990 exactly."

"Ah, that'd be right," says Paddy. "I knew I wasn't feeling two grand."

* * *

Maureen was having a consultation with her doctor. As they spoke, her son Tommy could clearly be heard terrorizing the people in the waiting room, yet she made no attempt to restrain him.

Soon they heard some clattering in an adjoining room, but still she did nothing. Finally, after an extra-loud crash, Maureen casually told the doctor, "I hope you don't mind my little Tommy playing in there?"

"No, not at all," said the doctor calmly. "I'm sure he'll calm down as soon as he finds the poison."

* * *

Vicky went to the doctor in a hell of a panic. "Doctor," she said, "I think I'm pregnant!"

"You can't be," replied the doctor, "Your husband had a vasectomy five years ago."

"That's why the panic!" she replied.

* * *

John walked into a bar and asked for a pint of less.

"Less?" questioned the barmaid. "I've never heard of it, is it a new beer?"

"I don't know," replied John. "I went to the doctor's this morning and he told me I should drink less."

* * *

A doctor and a lawyer were talking at a party. People describing their ailments and asking the doctor for free medical advice constantly interrupted their conversation. After an hour of this, the exasperated doctor asked the lawyer, "What do you do to stop people from asking you for legal advice when you're out of the office?"

"I give it to them," replied the lawyer, "and then I send them a bill." The doctor was shocked, but agreed to give it a try.

The next day, still feeling slightly guilty, the doctor prepared the bills. When he went to place them in his mailbox, he found a bill from the lawyer.

* * *

Antony goes to see his doctor and says, "Doctor, my sex life is terrible, absolutely terrible!" The doctor examines him and says, "You need exercise. I want you to run two miles every day. It'll improve your heart rate and your libido. Call me in a week."

A week later, Antony calls his doctor. "Well, Doc, I've been running two miles every day, just like you said."

The doctor asks him, "And how's your sex life now?"

Antony says, "I don't know, I'm 14 miles from home!"

* * *

Marie accompanied her husband Mark to the doctor's surgery. After his check-up, the doctor called Marie into his office alone. He said, "Mark is suffering from a very severe disease, combined with terrible stress. If you don't do the following, he will surely die. Each morning, fix him a healthy breakfast. Be pleasant, and make sure he is in a good mood. For lunch make him a nutritious meal. For dinner prepare an especially nice meal for him. Don't burden him with housework, as he has probably had a hard day. Don't discuss your problems with him; it will only make his stress worse. And most importantly, make love with your husband several times a week and satisfy his every whim. If you can do this for the next ten months to a year, I think Mark will be a new man and regain his health completely."

On the way home, Mark asked his wife, "What did the doctor say?"

"You're going to die," Marie replied.

* * *

Megan goes to the doctor and asks for his help to revive her husband's sex drive.

"What about trying Viagra?" asks the doctor.

"Not a chance," says Megan. "He won't even take an aspirin for a headache."

"No problem," replies the doctor. "Drop it into his coffee, he won't even taste it. Try it and come back in a week to let me know how you got on."

A week later Megan returns to the doctor and he inquires as to how things went.

"Oh it was terrible, just terrible doctor."

"What happened?" asks the doctor.

"Well I did as you advised and slipped it in his coffee. The effect was immediate. He jumped straight up, swept the cutlery off the table, at the same time ripping my clothes off and then proceeded to make passionate love to me on the tabletop. It was terrible."

"What was terrible?" asked the doctor, "was the sex not good?"

"Oh no doctor, the sex was the best I've had in 25 years. But I'll never be able to show my face in the National Milk Bar again!"

* * *

A doctor had just finished a marathon sex session with one of his patients. He was resting afterwards and was feeling a bit guilty because he thought it wasn't really ethical to screw one of his patients. However, a little voice in his head said, "Lots of other doctors have sex with their patients, so it's not like you're the first."

This made the doctor feel a little bit better until another voice in his head said, "but they probably weren't veterinarians."

* * *

"I went to a private doctor who said he would have me back on my feet in two weeks."

"And did he?"

"Yes, I had to sell the car to pay the bill!"

* * *

Tom says to the family doctor, "Doctor, I think my wife's going deaf."

The doctor answers, "Well, here's something you can try on her to test her hearing. Stand some distance away from her and ask her a question. If she doesn't answer, move a little closer and ask again. Keep repeating it until she answers. Then you'll be able to tell just how hard of hearing she really is."

Tom goes home and tries it out. He walks in the door and says, "Darling, what's for dinner?" He doesn't hear an answer, so he moves closer to her. "Darling, what's for dinner?" Still no answer. He repeats this several times, until he's standing just a few feet away from her.

Finally, she answers, "For the eleventh time, I said we're having roast chicken!"

* * *

John walks into a doctor's office and stutters, "Da-da-doc, I've ba-ba-been sta-sta-stuttering for ye-ye-years, and I ca-ca-can't stand it anymo-mo-more! Can you he-he-help me?" The doctor answers, "Well, I'll have to give you a thorough examination first, but in some cases there is a cure."

So the doctor puts John through a series of tests, and says, "I think I know what's causing your stuttering." John excitedly asks, "Well, wa-wa-what is it, da- da-doctor?"

"It's your penis. I know that sounds crazy, but you have an unusually large penis – it's almost two feet long. It seems the weight is putting a strain on your vocal cords which most men never have to deal with." John asks, "Wa-wa-what can we da-da-do?"

"Well, we could remove it and transplant a shorter one."

"Do it!" John replies. So they go through the operation, and three weeks later John comes in for a follow-up appointment.

He says, "Doc, you solved my stuttering problem. I don't know how to thank you. But I've only had sex once in three weeks. My wife just doesn't like it any more with my new shorter penis. I've thought about it, and I've decided I can put up with the stuttering easier than going without the sex. I want you to put my long one back on."

The doctor says, "No-no-nope. A da-da-deal's a da-da-deal!"

* * *

Bob sees his doctor and tells him that his wife has refused to have sex with him for the past seven months. The doctor tells Bob to bring his wife in so he can talk to her. So she goes in and the doctor asks her what's wrong, and why didn't she want to have sex with Bob anymore.

The wife tells him, "Every morning for the last seven months I've taken a cab to work. I don't have any money so the cab driver asks me, 'So are you going to pay today or what?' so I take a 'or what'. When I get to work I'm late so the boss asks me, 'So are we going to write this down in the book or what?' so I take a 'or what'. I take the cab home and again I don't have any money, so the cab driver asks me again, 'So are you going to pay this time or what?' so again I take a 'or what'. So you see doc, when I get home I'm all tired out, and I don't want it anymore."

The doctor thinks for a second and then turns to the wife and says, "So are we going to tell Bob or what?"

* * *

Ivan Jones gets home from work one day and finds his wife Janet has been crying. "What's wrong?" he asks.

"Ivan, promise you won't get mad, but I went to see the new doctor today and he told me I've got a pretty pussy."

"WHAT?" he shouts. With that he grabs a baseball bat from the cupboard and storms down to the doctor's office and through the reception area. Without knocking he bursts into the doctor's office. Ivan charges up to the doctor, smashes the baseball bat down on the desk and says, "You flaming pervert! How dare you say Janet has a pretty pussy?"

The doctor replies, "I'm sorry Mr Jones, but there has been a misunderstanding. I only told Janet that she has Acute Angina."

* * *

Tommy is a young boy, just potty trained. When he goes to the bathroom, though, Tommy manages to hit everything but the toilet. So his mother has to go in and clean up after him. After two weeks, she has had enough, and takes Tommy to the doctor.

After the examination, the doctor says, "His penis is too small. An old wives' tale is to give him two slices of toast each morning, and his penis will grow so he can hold it and aim straight."

The next morning Tommy jumped out of bed and ran downstairs to the kitchen. There on the table are twelve slices of toast.

"Mummy!" Tommy yells. "The doctor said I only had to eat two slices of toast."

"I know," said his mother. "The other ten are for your father."

* * *

One afternoon, Tony went to his doctor and told him that he hasn't been feeling well lately. The doctor examined the man, left the room, and came back with three different bottles of pills.

The doctor said, "Take the green pill with a big glass of water when you wake up. Take the blue pill with a big glass of water after you eat lunch. Then just before going to bed, take the red pill with another big glass of water."

Startled to be put on so much medicine, Tony stammered, "Bloody hell, doctor, exactly what is my problem?"

The doctor replied, "You're not drinking enough water."

* * *

David wasn't too happy with his doctor's recommendation to cure his constant fatigue.

"You want me to give up sex completely, Doc?" he cried. "I'm a young chap. I'm in the prime of my life. How do you expect me to give up sex and go cold turkey?"

"Well," replied the doctor, "you could get married and taper off gradually."

* * *

Selwyn had completed medical school. He went back home to work with his father. They went out the first day to make house calls. As they went into the first house the father said, "Now you watch me, so you will know what to do."

Inside, a woman was in bed and she looked terrible. The old doctor checked her out. He was making notes when he dropped his pen to the floor.

He picked it up and told the woman she needed to quit cleaning and working so hard in her house, and she just needed rest.

When they got outside, Selwyn asked how he knew that she was cleaning too much. The old doctor said that when he dropped his pen, the floor was so clean that there wasn't a speck of dust anywhere.

When they arrived at the next house, the father told Selwyn that it was his turn to examine the patient. At this house too, the woman was in bed, looking terrible. The young Selwyn took her blood pressure and pulse, asked a few questions, and made some notes. Then he dropped his pen and reached down to pick it up. He told the woman that she was doing too much church work, and needed to cut down on what she did.

When the two doctors went outside, the old doctor asked his son how he knew that she was doing too much church work.

Selwyn said, "Well, when I bent down to pick up my pen, I saw the preacher under the bed."

* * *

Sonia went to the doctor complaining of terribly bad knee pains. After the diagnostic tests showed nothing, the doctor questioned her. "There must be something you're doing that you haven't told me about. Can you think of anything that might be doing this to your knees?"

"Well," Sonia said a little sheepishly, "Gareth and I have sex doggy-style on the floor every night."

"That's got to be it," said the doctor. "There are plenty of other positions and ways to have sex, you know."

"Not if you're going to watch television, there ain't!" Sonia replied.

* * *

An attractive young girl, chaperoned by an ugly old crone, entered the doctor's office. "We have come for an examination," said the young girl.

"Alright," said the doctor. "Go behind that curtain and take your clothes off."

"No, not me," said the girl. "It's my old aunt here."

"Very well… Madam, put your tongue out."

* * *

There was a businessman who was not feeling well, so he went to see the doctor about it. The doctor said to him, "Well, it must be your diet. What sort of greens do you eat?"

The man replied, "Well, actually, I only eat peas, I hate all other green foods." The doctor was quite shocked at this and said, "Well man, that's your problem, all those peas will be clogging up your system. You'll have to give them up!!"

The guy said, "But how long for, I mean I really like peas!"

The doctor replied, "Forever, I'm afraid."

The man was quite shocked by this, but he gave it a go and sure enough, his condition improved, so he resolved that he would never eat a pea again.

Anyway, one night, years later, he was at a convention for his employer and getting quite sloshed and one of the reps said, "Well, ashully, I'd love a cigarette, coz I avint ad a smoke in four years. I gave it up."

The barman goes, "Really? I haven't had a game of golf in three years, because it cost me my first marriage, so I gave it up!"

The businessman says, "Thas nuvving, I haven't ad a pea in six years," and the barman jumps up screaming, "Okay, everyone who can't swim, grab a table…"

* * *

John goes to a doctor and says he has a problem with sex. "I think my privates are too small," he says. The doctor asks him which drink he prefers.

"Well, lager," he replies, quite bemused.

"Ah! There's your problem. They shrink things, those lagers. You should try drinking Guinness. That makes things grow."

Two months later John returns to the doctor with a big smile on his face. He shakes the doctor by the hand and thanks him.

"I take it you now drink Guinness?" asked the doc.

"Yes," replies John. "But I've also got the wife on lager!"

* * *

Dr Thomas and his wife were having a heated argument at breakfast. As he stormed out of the house, he yelled angrily to his wife, "You aren't that good in bed either!"

By mid-morning, Dr Thomas decided he'd better make up and phoned home. After many rings, his wife – clearly out of breath – answered the phone.

"What took you so long to answer and why are you panting?"

"I was in bed," she said.

"What in the world are you doing in bed at this hour?"

"Getting a second opinion."

* * *

After suffering from severe headaches for years with no relief, Trevor is referred to a headache specialist by his family GP.

"The trouble is," Trevor tells the specialist, "I get this blinding pain, like a knife across my scalp and…" He is interrupted by the doctor, "And a heavy throbbing right behind the left ear?"

"Yes! Exactly! How did you know?"

"Well, I myself suffered from that same type of headache for many years. It is caused by a tension in the scalp muscles. This is how I cured it: every day I would give my wife oral sex."

"Is that all it takes?" says Trevor, intrigued.

"Oh no," says the doctor. "When she came she would squeeze her legs together with all her strength and the pressure would relieve the tension in my head. Try that every day for two weeks and come back and let me know how it goes."

Two weeks go by and Trevor returns, grinning, "Doc, I'm a new man! I haven't had a headache since I started the treatment. I can't thank you enough."

"That's fine," says the doctor, "I was glad to pass on a personal cure."

"By the way," says Trevor, standing to leave, "You have a lovely home."

* * *

Bethany goes for a check-up. She seems to be very embarrassed and uncomfortable.

"Haven't you been examined like this before?" asks the doctor.

"Many times," she giggles, "but never by a doctor!"

* * *

Mrs Davies went to see her doctor. When he inquired about her complaint she replied that she suffered from a discharge. The doctor said, "Get undressed, Mrs Davies, and lie down on the examining table." She did, whereupon the doctor put on rubber gloves and began to massage her private parts.

After a couple of minutes he asked, "How does that feel?"

"Wonderful," Mrs Davies replied, "but the discharge is from my ear!"

Hospital Doctors

John, as a young lad, went into hospital for some minor surgery, and the day after the procedure a friend stopped by to see how he was doing. His friend was amazed at the number of nurses who entered the room in short intervals with refreshments, offers to fluff his pillows, make the bed, give back rubs, etc.

"Why all the attention?" the friend asked, "You look fine to me."

"I know!" grinned, John. "But the nurses kind of formed a little fan club when they all heard that my circumcision required 27 stitches."

* * *

A husband was just coming out of anaesthesia after having surgery, and his faithful wife was sitting at his bedside.

His eyes started to open and he quietly uttered, "You're beautiful."

He soon drifted back to sleep, and after awhile he woke up and said, "You're cute."

"What happened to beautiful?" she asked him.

"The drugs are wearing off," he replied.

* * *

An old farmer had to go into hospital for an operation. As soon as he arrived at the hospital he was given a good bath by the nurses. As he left the bathroom he said to one of them, "Well, I'm glad that's over. I've been dreading that operation for years."

* * *

A doctor pulls out a thermometer from his shirt pocket. He looks at it and says, "Shit, some arsehole has nicked my pen!!!"

* * *

Sonia goes to the hospital, complaining that she is exhausted all the time. After the diagnostic tests showed nothing, the doctor gets around to asking her how often she has intercourse.

"Every Monday, Wednesday, and Saturday," she says.

The doctor advises her to cut out Wednesdays.

"I can't," she says. "That's the only night I'm home with my husband."

* * *

At an international meeting, two surgeons were having an argument. The Indian surgeon says, "No no no, I am telling you it is 'woomba'."

The African surgeon says, "No, Man, it is 'whoooooommmmmm'."

They go on like this for about ten minutes. Up comes the English surgeon and interrupts them.

"Excuse me chaps, but I do believe that the word you are trying to say is 'womb'."

After he has gone away, the African turns to the Indian and says, "I bet you he has never even *seen* an elephant, never mind heard one fart!"

* * *

After days of abdominal pain, Thomas goes to the hospital for some tests. Returning a few weeks later, he asks for the results.

"Hmm," says the specialist, looking up from his paperwork. "I have some good news and some bad news."

Thomas is visibly concerned. "I suppose I'd better have the good news first."

"Well," sighs the specialist, "We're going to name the disease after you."

* * *

Nigel goes into the hospital for a vasectomy. Shortly after he recovers from his anaesthetic, his surgeon comes in and tells him, "Well Nigel, I've got good news and I've got bad news for you."

"Give me the bad news first, Doc," replies Nigel.

"I'm afraid that we accidentally cut your balls off during surgery, son."

"Oh my god!" Nigel cries, breaking into tears.

"But the good news," the doctor adds, "is that we did a biopsy and you'll be relieved to know that they weren't malignant!"

* * *

Five doctors went duck hunting one day. Included in the group were a GP, a paediatrician, a psychiatrist, a surgeon and a pathologist.

After a time, a bird came winging overhead. The first to react was the GP who raised his shotgun, but then hesitated.

"I'm not quite sure it's a duck," he said, "I think that I will have to get a second opinion." And of course by that time, the bird was long gone.

Another bird appeared in the sky thereafter. This time, the paediatrician raised his gun. He too, however, was unsure if it was really a duck in his sights and besides, it might have babies. "I'll have to do some more investigations," he muttered, as the creature made good its escape.

Next to spy a bird flying was the sharp-eyed psychiatrist. Shotgun shouldered, he was more certain of his intended prey's identity. "Now, I know it's a duck, but does *it* know it's a duck?" The fortunate bird disappeared while the fellow wrestled with this dilemma.

Finally, a fourth fowl sped past, and this time the

surgeon's weapon pointed skywards. BOOM!!

The surgeon lowered his smoking gun and turned nonchalantly to the pathologist beside him and said, "Go see if that was a duck, will you?"

* * *

John is plagued by terrible headaches. One day, after years of suffering, he decides to see a specialist. The doctor tells John to strip, inspects him all over, and announces that he's found the cause of his problem.

"Your testicles are pressing against the base of your spine," says the medic. "The pressure builds up, and you get an excruciating headache."

John is appalled. "Tell me, doctor, is there anything I can do about it?" he asks.

The doctor replies, "I'm afraid I have bad news. The only answer is to get rid of the testicles."

John considers the pros and cons of a life without balls and sex – but then he thinks about the agony of his daily headaches, and without too much difficulty decides to go for the snip.

He comes round from the operation and leaves the hospital. Walking along the street, he smiles and realizes that the pain has completely disappeared. To celebrate, he decides to treat himself to some new clothes, so he makes his way to a top tailor to get fitted.

Inside the tailor's, he asks to see a pair of trousers.

The tailor looks at John and says, "You'll need a 36-inch waist, 33-inch inside leg." John is amazed at the accuracy of the tailor's eye, and asks for a shirt.

"That'll be a 42-inch chest, 16-inch neck," the tailor says, and John is once again stunned by his accuracy.

Finally, all that is left is a pair of underpants.

"36?" guesses the tailor – incorrectly.

"No, sorry, I'm 34," John says, "I've worn a 34 since I was 18."

"That's not possible," frowns the tailor. "If a man of your size wore a size 34, the pants would press his testicles into the base of his spine, causing the most horrific headaches."

* * *

There is a knock on St Peter's door. He looks out and a man is standing there. St Peter is about to begin his interview when the man disappears.

A short time later there's another knock. St Peter gets the door, sees the man, opens his mouth to speak, and the man disappears once again.

A few minutes later, another knock. Once again St Peter opens the door and sees the same man. "Hey, are you playing games with me?" St Peter calls after him.

"No," the man's distant voice replies anxiously. "They're trying to resuscitate me."

* * *

A college physics professor was explaining a particularly complicated concept to his class when a medical student interrupted him.

"Why do we have to learn this stuff?" the young man blurted out.

"To save lives," the professor responded before continuing the lecture.

A few minutes later the student spoke up again. "So how does physics save lives?"

The professor stared at the student for a long time without saying a word. Finally the professor continued. "Physics saves lives," he said, "because it keeps the idiots out of medical school."

* * *

Feeling anxious, Dave decided to take a hot bath. Just as he became comfortable, the doorbell rang. Dave got out of the tub, put on his slippers and robe and went to answer the door.

It was a door-to-door salesman, asking if he needed any brushes. Slamming the door, Dave returned to the bath.

The doorbell rang again. On went the slippers and robe, and Dave started for the door again. He took one step, slipped on a wet spot, fell backward, and hit his back against the hard porcelain bathtub. Cursing under his breath Dave struggled into his street clothes and with every move causing a stab of pain, drove to the doctor.

After examining him, the doctor said, "You know Dave, you've been lucky. Nothing's broken. But you need to relax… Why don't you go home and take a long hot bath?"

* * *

Sonia goes to the dentist. In the chair, the dentist notices a little brown spot on one of her teeth.

"Aha, a cavity! I'll have to drill this one out!" says the dentist.

"Oh, no – not a filling, I'd rather have a baby!" cries Sonia.

"In that case, I'll have to adjust the chair first," replies the dentist.

* * *

Then there's Sue who goes to the dentist. As he leans over to begin working on her, she grabs his balls.

The dentist says, "Madam, I believe you've got a hold of my privates."

She replies, "Aye… and we're going to be careful not to hurt each other, aren't we…"

* * *

"Darling, listen to me," pleaded her dentist. "We've got to stop this. It'll only end in tears."

"But why?" she asked. "We've had a great relationship for over a year and my husband's never found out. He's not even suspicious."

"But he will be soon. Don't you realise you've only got one tooth left?"

* * *

With the help of a fertility specialist, a 65-year-old woman has a baby. All her relatives come to visit and meet the newest member of their family. When they ask to see the baby, the mother says, "not yet."

A little later they ask to see the baby again. Again the mother says, "not yet." Finally they say, "When can we see the baby!?" And the mother says, "You'll have to wait until the baby cries."

And they ask, "Why do we have to wait until the baby cries?" The new mother says, "because I forgot where I put it!"

* * *

Vicky gives birth and afterwards the doctor comes in. He says, "Vicky, I have to tell you something about your baby."

Vicky sits up in bed and says, "What's wrong with my baby, Doctor? What's wrong?"

The doctor says, "Well Vicky, there's nothing's wrong, exactly, but your baby is a little bit different. Your baby is a hermaphrodite."

Vicky says, "A hermaphrodite? what's that?"

The doctor says, "Well, it means your baby has the... um... sort of... features... um... of a male and a female."

Vicky turns pale. She says, "Oh my God! You mean it has a penis... AND a brain!!!"

* * *

Marge goes to her doctor who verifies that she is pregnant. This is her first pregnancy. The doctor asks her if she has any questions.

Marge replies, "Well, I'm a little worried about the pain. How much will childbirth hurt?"

The doctor answered, "Well, that varies from woman to woman and pregnancy to pregnancy and besides, it's difficult to describe pain."

"I know, but can't you give me some idea?" she asks.

"Grab your upper lip and pull it out a little..."

"Like this?"

"A little more..."

"Like this?"

"No. A little more..."

"Like this?"

"Yes. Does that hurt?"

"A little bit."

"Now stretch it over your head!"

* * *

Vicky took her baby in to see the doctor, and he determined right away the baby had an earache. He wrote a prescription for ear drops. In the directions he wrote: 'Put two drops in right ear every four hours,' and he abbreviated 'right' as an R with a circle around it.

Several days passed, and Vicky returned with her baby, complaining that the baby still had an earache, and his little behind was getting really greasy with all those drops of oil.

The doctor looked at the bottle of ear drops and sure enough, the pharmacist had typed the following instructions on the label: 'Put two drops in R ear every four hours.'

* * *

At hospital, the relatives gathered in the waiting room, where their family member lay gravely ill. Finally, the doctor came in looking tired and sombre.

"I'm afraid I am the bearer of bad news," he said as he surveyed the worried faces, "The only hope left for your loved one at this time is a brain transplant. It's an experimental procedure, semi-risky, and you will have to pay for the brain yourselves."

The family members sat silent as they absorbed the news. After a length of time, someone asked, "Well, how much does a brain cost?" The doctor quickly responded, "£5,000 for a male brain, and £200 for a female brain."

The moment turned awkward. Men in the room tried not to smile, avoiding eye contact with the women, but some actually smirked. A man, unable to control his curiosity, blurted out the question everyone wanted to ask, "Why is the male brain so much more?"

The doctor smiled at the childish innocence and then to the entire group said, "It's just standard pricing procedure. We have to mark down the price of the female brains, because they've been used."

* * *

John goes to the doctor and says, "Doc, I would like to live very long. What should I do?"

"I think that is a wise decision," the doctor replies. "Let's see, do you smoke?"

"Oh, half a pack a day," John replied.

"Starting NOW, no more smoking." John agrees.

The doctor then asks, "Do you drink?"

"Oh, well Doc, not much, just a bit of wine with my meals, and a beer or two every once in a while."

"Starting now, you drink only water. No exceptions." John is a bit upset, but also agrees.

The doctor asks, "How do you eat?"

"Oh, well, you know, Doc, normal stuff," says John.

"Starting now you are going on a very strict diet: you are going to eat only raw vegetables, with no dressing, and non-fat cottage cheese."

John is now really worried.

"Doc, is all this really necessary?"

"Do you want to live long?"

"Yes."

"Absolutely necessary. And don't even think of breaking the diet."

John is quite restless, but the doctor continues, "Do you have sex?"

"Yeah, once a week or so. Only with Vicky!" he adds hurriedly.

"As soon as you get out of here you are going to buy twin beds. No more sex for you. None."

John is absolutely appalled. "Doc... Are you sure I'm going to live longer this way?"

"I have no idea, but however long you live, I assure you it is going to seem like an eternity!"

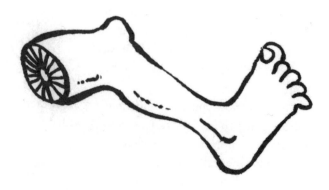

Doctor Doctor...

"Doctor, doctor, I think I'm a bell!"
"Take these, and if it doesn't help, give me a ring!"

"Doctor, doctor, I think I'm suffering from deja vu!"
"Didn't I see you yesterday?"

"Doctor, doctor, I've got wind! Can you give me
something?"
"Yes – here's a kite!"

"Doctor, doctor, you've got to help me – I just can't
stop my hands shaking."
"Do you drink a lot?"
"Not really – I spill most of it!"

"Doctor, doctor, I think I'm a bridge."
"What's come over you?"
"Oh, two cars, a large truck and a coach."

"Doctor, doctor, I feel like biscuits!"
"What, you mean those square ones?"
"Yes!"

"The ones you put butter on?"
"Yes!"
"Oh, you're crackers!"

"Doctor, doctor, can I have second opinion?"
"Of course, come back tomorrow!"

"Doctor, doctor, I keep thinking I'm a wicket-keeper."
"You've got me stumped!"

"Doctor, doctor, I keep thinking I'm John McEnroe."
"You cannot be serious!"

"Doctor, doctor, I keep thinking I'm Long John Silver."
"Let me have a look at your chest!"

"Doctor, doctor, everyone thinks I'm a liar."
"Well, I can't believe that!"

"Doctor, doctor, I tend to flush a lot."
"Don't worry it's just a chain reaction!"

"Doctor, doctor, you have to help me out!"
"Certainly, which way did you come in?"

"Doctor, doctor, all I can think of is gin, gin, gin."
"What you need is a tonic!"

"Doctor, doctor, are you sure this medicine will cure me?"
"Well, nobody's been back for a second bottle!"

"Doctor, doctor, every time I drink a cup of tea, I get a stabbing pain in my right eye."
"Try taking the spoon out of the cup first."

"Doctor, doctor, everyone keeps ignoring me."
"Next patient, please!"

"Doctor, doctor, everyone thinks I'm a cricket ball."
"How's that?"
"Not you as well!"

"Doctor, doctor, I believe I'm a disc jockey."
"Nonsense – you're just in a groove!"

"Doctor, doctor, I believe I'm a motor horn."
"I don't give a hoot!"

"Doctor, doctor, I get the feeling people don't care about anything I say."
"So…?"

"Doctor, doctor, I hate castor oil."
"You don't expect me to swallow that!"

"Doctor, doctor, I have trouble getting to sleep at nights."
"Lie on the edge of the bed – you'll soon drop off!"

"Doctor, doctor, I need something for my liver."
"Here's a pound of onions!"

"Doctor, doctor, I'm allergic to liquorice."
"Well, it takes allsorts to make a world!"

"Doctor, doctor, nobody takes me seriously."
"You're kidding!"

"Doctor, doctor, people take me for a beekeeper."
"Sit over here, honey!"

"Doctor, doctor, some days I feel like a tee-pee and other days I feel like a wig-wam."
"You're too tents!"

"Doctor, doctor, the Invisible Man is waiting outside."
"Tell him I can't see him!"

"Doctor, doctor, this banana diet you put me on is having a strange effect."
"Well, stop scratching and come down from the curtains!"

"Doctor, doctor, I feel like a billiard ball."
"Well, get to the back of the queue!"

"Doctor, doctor, I feel like a pair of curtains."
"Pull yourself together!"

"Doctor, doctor, I feel like a ten pound note."
"Go shopping – the change will do you good!"

"Doctor, doctor, I feel like a pack of cards."
"Please wait a minute, and I'll deal with you!"

"Doctor, doctor, I've swallowed the film from my camera."
"We'll just have to wait and see what develops!"

"Doctor, doctor, I keep thinking I'm a clock."
"OK, just relax. There's no need to get yourself wound up!"

"Doctor, doctor, I think I'm a dustbin."
"Now you're just talking rubbish!"

"Doctor, doctor, I keep thinking I'm a dog."
"Sit down and tell me all about it."
"I can't, I'm not allowed on the furniture!"

"Doctor, doctor, I've lost my memory."

"When did this happen?"
"When did what happen?"

"Doctor, doctor, I keep seeing little black spots before my eyes."
"Have you seen a doctor before?"
"No, just little black spots!"

Doctor: "We need to get these people to a hospital!"
Nurse: "What is it?"
Doctor: "It's a big building with a lot of doctors!"

Doctor: "Nurse, how is that little boy doing, the one who swallowed ten pounds?"
Nurse: "No change yet!"

Patient: "My hair keeps falling out. What can you give me to keep it in?"
Doctor: "A shoebox!"

Patient: "Doctor, should I file my nails?"
Doctor: "No, throw them away like everybody else!"

"Doctor, doctor, Have you got something for a bad headache?"
"Of course. Just take this hammer and hit yourself in the head. Then you'll have a bad headache!"
"Doctor, doctor, I keep seeing double."

"Please sit on the couch."
"Which one?"

"Doctor, doctor, I'm having trouble with my
breathing."
"I'll give you something that will soon put a stop to
that!"

"Doctor, doctor, I've broke my arm in two places."
"Well don't go back there again, then!"

"Doctor, doctor, will this ointment clear up my spots?"
"I never make rash promises!"

"Doctor, doctor, you've taken out my tonsils, my
adenoids, my gall bladder, my varicose veins and my
appendix, but I still don't feel well."
"That's quite enough out of you!"

"Doctor, doctor, my baby is the image of his father."
"Never mind, just so long as he's healthy!"

"Doctor, doctor, my sister here keeps thinking she's
invisible."
"What sister?"

"Doctor, doctor, my sister thinks she is a lift!"
"Well, tell her to come in."

"I can't – she doesn't stop at this floor!"

"Doctor, doctor, my daughter thinks she's an actress."
"Don't worry – it's just a stage she's going through!"

"Doctor, doctor, my eleven-year-old son weighs fifteen stone and is seven feet tall."
"Don't worry – he'll grow out of it."

"Doctor, doctor, my husband thinks he's a car."
"Show him in at once."
"I can't – he's double parked!"

"Doctor, doctor, my husband thinks I'm mad because I like kippers."
"That's nonsense. I like kippers too."
"Really? You must come round and see my collection!"

"Doctor, doctor, my husband thinks he's Moses."
"Tell him to stop taking the tablets!"

"Doctor, doctor, my husband thinks he's a parachutist."
"Tell him to drop in and see me!"

Doctor : "Are you on HRT?"
Patient : "No, income support!"

Man: Doctor, me leg keeps talkin' to me.

Doc: Don't be ridiculous!

Leg: Lend us a fiver!

Man: Told ya.

Leg: Giz a tenner!

Doc: My God!

Leg: Hey Doc, can you spare 20 quid?

Doc: I know your problem. Your leg's broke!

Nurses

Taken from some answers in a trainee nurse entrance exam.

"Three kinds of blood vessels are arteries, vanes and caterpillars."

"The body consists of three parts – the branium, the borax, and the abominable cavity. The branium contains the brain, the borax contains the heart and lungs, and the abominable cavity contains the bowels, of which there are five – a, e, i, o and u."

"Blood flows down one leg and up the other."

"Respiration is composed of two acts, first inspiration, and then expectoration."

Q: What happens to your body as you age?
A: When you get old, so do your bowels and you get intercontinental.

Q: What happens to a boy when he reaches puberty?

A: He says goodbye to his boyhood and looks forward to his adultery.

Q: Name a major disease associated with cigarettes.
A: Premature death.

Q: How can you delay milk turning sour?
A. Keep it in the cow.

Q: What is the Fibula?
A: A small lie.

Q: What does 'varicose' mean?
A: Nearby.

Q: What is the most common form of birth control?
A: Most people prevent contraception by wearing a condominium.

Q: Give the meaning of the term 'Caesarean Section.'
A: The caesarean section is a district in Rome.

Q: What is a seizure?
A: A Roman emperor.

Q: What is a terminal illness?
A: When you are sick at the airport.

Q: Give an example of a fungus. What is a characteristic feature?
A: Mushrooms. They always grow in damp places and so they look like umbrellas.

* * *

A hospital posted a notice in the nurse's lounge saying, 'Remember, the first five minutes of a human being's life are the most dangerous.' Underneath, a nurse had written: 'The last five are pretty risky, too.'

* * *

Matthew is involved in a terrible cycling accident, in which he breaks all of his limbs. Waking up in hospital several days later, his legs hoisted in the air and his arms encased in plaster, he finds the doctor looking at him from a chair next to his bed.

"Oh," the doctor says, "you're awake. How do you feel, my man?"

"Considering I've had such a terrible accident, I really don't feel too bad," the injured Matthew replies. "In fact, I feel pretty bloody good."

But as he finishes saying this, he suddenly leans to his left. The doctor, realizing Matthew has no means of support, grabs him and props him upright.

Later on a nurse comes by to check on him and asks him how he's getting on.

"As I said earlier," the injured Matthew says, "when

you consider what I've been through I actually feel super." And again, he begins to fall to one side. The nurse jumps forward and sits him upright, then goes on her way.

The next day, Matthew's wife comes in and asks him how he's feeling.

"As I've told everyone," he says, "I feel fine. I just wish these bastards would let me fart in comfort."

* * *

Did you hear about the nurse who died and went straight to hell?

It took her two weeks to realize that she wasn't at work anymore!

* * *

A nurse caring for John asked him, "So how's your breakfast this morning?"

"It's very good, except for the Kentucky Jelly. I can't seem to get used to the taste," John replied. The nurse asked to see the jelly and John produced a foil packet labelled 'KY Jelly.'

* * *

Plain nurse to pretty nurse: "Have you seen John in Ward Three? He's tatooed all over! I was giving him a bath this morning and I noticed he's even got 'Ludo' tattooed on his you-know-what."

Pretty nurse: "That's not 'Ludo', that's 'Llandudno'!"

* * *

Welsh health lecturer in a seminar to some nurses: "The two most debilitating diseases in Wales are silicosis and syphilis. Silicosis you get by going down a shaft."

* * *

Sister Thelma looked up and saw the young nurse holding a kettle as one of the patients came screaming down the ward. She shouted, "No, Nurse Thomas, I told you to prick his boil!"

* * *

John was hospitalised, and was always rather rude to his nurses. Being a very bossy sort of chap, he always ordered them around as if they were his employees. But the Ward Sister stood up to him.

One morning she entered the Ward and told him, "I have to take your temperature." After complaining for several minutes, he finally settled down, crossed his arms and opened his mouth.

"No, I'm sorry," the Sister stated, "For this reading, I can't use an oral thermometer." This started another round of complaining, but eventually he rolled over and bared his bottom. After feeling the Sister insert the thermometer, he heard her say, "I have to get something. Now you stay just like that until I get back!" She left the curtains open on her way out, and John cursed under his breath as he heard people walking past his bed laughing. After almost an hour, John's doctor came to the bedside.

"What's going on here?" asked the doctor.

Angrily, John answered, "What's the matter, Doc? Haven't you ever seen someone having their temperature taken?"

"Yes," replied the doctor. "But never with a carnation."

* * *

"How come you're late?" asked the ward manager, as Vicky, the nursing assistant, walked into work.

"It was awful," Vicky explained. "I was walking down Bridge Street and there was a terrible accident. A man was thrown from his car and he was lying in the middle of the street. His leg was broken, his skull was fractured, and there was blood everywhere. Thank God I took that first aid course."

"What did you do?" asked the ward manager.

"I sat down and put my head between my knees to keep from fainting!"

* * *

A memo sent to Human Resources:

Dear Human Resources,

Mary Jones, my S.R.N., can always be found
hard at work in her station. Mary works independently, without
wasting hospital time talking to colleagues. Mary never
thinks twice about assisting fellow nurses, and she always
finishes given tasks on time. Often, Mary takes extended
measures to complete her work, sometimes skipping coffee
breaks. Mary is an individual who has absolutely no
vanity in spite of her high accomplishments and profound
knowledge in her field. I firmly believe that Mary can be
classed as a high-calibre employee, the type which cannot be
dispensed with. Consequently, I duly recommend that Mary be
promoted to executive management, and a proposal will be
executed as soon as possible.

   Regards - Charge Nurse

Shortly thereafter, the Human Resources department received the following memo from the Charge Nurse:

Sorry, but that idiot (Mary) was reading over my
shoulder while I wrote the report sent to you
earlier today. Kindly read only the odd numbered
lines for my true assessment of her.

* * *

A nurse was leaving hospital one evening when she found a doctor standing in front of a shredder with a piece of paper in his hand.

"Listen," said the doctor, "this is important and my assistant has left. Can you make this thing work?"

"Certainly," said the nurse, flattered that the doctor had asked her for help.

She turned the machine on, inserted the paper and pressed the start button.

"Excellent! Excellent!" said the doctor as his paper disappeared inside the machine. "I need two copies of that."

* * *

A lady came to the hospital to visit a friend. She had not been in a hospital for several years and felt very ignorant about all the new technology. A technician followed her onto the elevator, wheeling a large, intimidating looking machine with tubes and wires and dials.

"Boy, would I hate to be hooked up to that thing," she said.

"So would I," replied the technician. "It's a floor-cleaning machine."

* * *

Three nurses go into the morgue, and there's Dave, laying dead there, with an erection. The first nurse sees it and says, "I'm gagging for it," then she gets on top of Dave and has her way with him. The second nurse says, "Aye, so am I, shame to let it go to waste," and she does the same. They turn to the third nurse, and ask her if she is having a go. She replied that she is having her period and declines. One of the nurses says, "Dave's dead anyway – he'll not be bothered." The last nurse agrees with this, gets on and does her thing too.

Just after she finishes, Dave sits up. The nurses tell him, "We thought you were dead!" and Dave replied, "After two jump starts and a blood transfusion, you wouldn't be dead either!"

* * *

One day Nurse Jones had to be the bearer of bad news when she told a woman that her husband had died of a massive myocardial infarction. Not more that five minutes later, she heard the woman reporting to the rest of the family that he had died of a "massive internal fart."

* * *

Bob goes to a doctor for a medical. When he gets into the room, he strips for his examination. He has a member the size of a little kid's little finger. The nurse standing in the room sees his little member and begins to laugh hysterically. Bob gives her a stern look and says, "You shouldn't laugh, it's been swollen like this for two weeks now!"

* * *

Two nurses were talking about the new hunk in the ward.

"But he acts so stupid," said one nurse to the other. "I think he must have his brains between his legs."

"Yeah," her colleague sighed, "but I'd sure love to blow his mind."

* * *

Top ten reasons to become a nurse:

1) Pays better than fast food, though the hours aren't as good.
2) Fashionable shoes and sexy white uniforms.
3) Needles: "Tis better to give than receive."
4) Reassure your patients that all bleeding stops… eventually.
5) Expose yourself to rare, exciting and new diseases.
6) Interesting aromas.
7) Courteous and infallible doctors who always leave clear orders in perfectly legible handwriting.
8) Do enough charting to navigate around the world.
9) Celebrate all the holidays with your friends – at work.
10) Take comfort that most of your patients survive, no matter what you do to them.

* * *

You know you're a nurse if:

- You believe not all patients are annoying... some are unconscious.
- Your sense of humour seems to get more warped each year.
- You can only tell time with a 24-hour clock.
- Almost everything can seem humorous... eventually.
- When asked, "What colour is the patient's diarrhoea?" you show them your shoes.
- You can tell the pharmacist more about the medicines he is dispensing than he can.
- You check the caller ID when the phone rings on your day off to see if someone from the hospital is trying to call to ask you to work.
- You've been telling stories in a restaurant and caused someone at another table throw up.
- You notice that you use more four-letter words now than before you became a nurse.
- Every time someone asks you for a pen, you can find at least three of them on you.
- You don't get excited about blood loss... unless it's your own.
- You've told a confused patient your name was that of your co-worker and to shout if they need help.

- You find yourself checking out other customers' arm veins in grocery waiting lines.

- You can sleep soundly at the hospital cafeteria table during dinner break sitting up and not be embarrassed when you wake up.

- You avoid unhealthy looking shoppers in the mall for fear that they'll drop near you and you'll have to do CPR on your day off.

* * *

A nursing assistant, staff nurse, and sister from a small nursing home were taking a lunch break. In walked a lady dressed in silk scarves and wearing large polished stoned jewellery.

"I am Gina the Great," stated the lady. "I am so pleased with the way you have taken care of my aunt that I will now grant you three wishes!" With a wave of her hand and a puff of smoke, the room was filled with flowers, fruit and bottles of drink, proving that she did have the power to grant wishes, before any of the nurses could think otherwise. The nurses quickly argued among themselves as to which one would ask for the first wish. Speaking up, the nursing assistant wished first.

"I wish I were on a tropical island beach, with single, well-built men feeding me fruit and tending to my every need." With a puff of smoke, the nursing assistant was gone.

The staff nurse went next. "I wish I were rich and retired and spending my days in my own warm cabin at a ski resort with well-groomed men feeding me cocoa and doughnuts." With a puff of smoke, she too was gone.

"Now, what is the last wish?" asked the lady.

The sister said, "I want those two back on the floor at the end of the lunch break."

Patients

Code of Ethical Patient Behaviour

1. Do not expect your doctor to share your discomfort. Involvement with the patient's suffering might cause him to lose valuable scientific objectivity.

2. Be cheerful at all times. Your doctor leads a busy and trying life and requires all the gentleness and reassurance he can get.

3. Try to suffer from the disease for which you are being treated. Remember that your doctor has a professional reputation to uphold.

4. Do not complain if the treatment fails to bring relief. You must believe that your doctor has achieved a deep insight into the true nature of your illness, which transcends any mere permanent disability you may have experienced.

5. Never ask your doctor to explain what he is doing or why he is doing it. It is presumptuous to assume that such profound matters could be explained in terms that you would understand.

6. Pay your medical bills promptly and willingly. You should consider it a privilege to contribute, however modestly, to the well-being of physicians, health care managers and other humanitarians.

7. Do not suffer from ailments not covered by your health care plan. It is a waste of resources to contract illnesses that are beyond your means.

8. Never reveal any of the shortcomings that have come to light in the course of treatment by your doctor. The patient-doctor relationship is a privileged one and you have a sacred duty to protect him from exposure.

9. Never die while in your doctor's presence or under his direct care. This will only cause him needless inconvenience and embarrassment.

* * *

Vicky is in hospital, recovering from an appendicitis operation, and is being visited by her colleague Sian.

"How are things at the office, Jane?" she asked.

"Well," replied Jane, "we're all sharing your work. Marge is making the coffee, Beth is doing the photocopying, Sharon is doing the typing, I'm reading your magazines, and Brenda is shagging the boss!"

* * *

Following a nasty car accident, John's wife Vicky slips into a coma. After spending weeks at her bedside, John is summoned to the hospital.

"It's amazing," says the doctor, breathlessly. "While bathing your wife, one of the nurses noticed she responded to her breasts being touched." John is very excited, and asks what he can do.

"Well," says the doc, "if one erogenous zone provokes a response, perhaps the others will too."
So John goes alone into the room, where he slips his hand under the covers and begins to massage her bits. Amazingly, Vicky begins to move and even moan a little. John tells the doctor, waiting outside.

"Excellent!" he says. "If she responds like that to your finger, I think you should try oral sex." Nodding, John returns to the room – but within minutes the heart monitor alarms go off, and the medics pile into the room.

"What happened?" shouts the doctor, as he checks the prone woman's pulse.

"I'm not sure," replies John, looking sheepish. "I think she choked."

* * *

Gareth was in a terrible accident, and his manhood was mangled and torn from his body. His doctor assured him that modern medicine could give him back his manhood, but that his insurance wouldn't cover the surgery, since it was considered cosmetic. The doctor said the cost would be £3,500 for small,

£6,500 for medium and £14,000 for large. Gareth was sure he would want a medium or large, but the doctor urged him to talk it over with his wife Bethan before he made any decision. Gareth called Bethan on the phone and explained their options. The doctor came back into the room, and found Gareth looking dejected.

"Well, what have the two of you decided?"

Gareth answered, "Bethan would rather have a new kitchen."

* * *

A nursing assistant was helping John into the bathroom when John exclaimed, "You're not coming in here with me. This is only a one-seater!"

* * *

Dave and John were talking from their hospital beds when Dave turns to John saying, "John, if I should die first, will you pour a gallon of beer over my grave?"

"No problem," says John, "as long as you don't mind if it goes through my kidneys first!"

* * *

The room was full of pregnant women and their partners, and the class was in full swing. The instructor was teaching the women how to breathe properly, along with informing the men how to give the necessary assurances at this stage of the plan.

The teacher then announced, "Ladies, exercise is good for you. Walking is especially beneficial. And, gentlemen, it wouldn't hurt you to take the time to go walking with your partner!"

The room got quiet. Finally, a man in the middle of the group raised his hand. "Yes?" asked the teacher.

"Is it all right if she carries a golf bag while we walk?"

* * *

Q. What's the fastest way to a man's heart?
A. Through his chest with a sharp knife.

* * *

The owner of a pharmacy arrives at work to find a man leaning heavily against a wall. The owner goes inside and asks his assistant what's up.

"He wanted something for his cough, but I couldn't find the cough syrup," the clerk explains. "So I gave him a laxative and told him to take it all at once."

"Laxatives won't cure a cough, you idiot," the owner shouts angrily.

"Sure it will," the assistant says, pointing at the man leaning on the wall. "Look at him. He's afraid to cough."

* * *

Once upon a time there was a female brain cell which, by mistake, happened to end up in a man's head. She looked around nervously because it was all empty and quiet. "Hello?" she cried, but no answer. "Is anyone here?" she cried a little louder, but still no answer. Now the female brain cell started to feel alone and scared and yelled at the top of her voice, "HELLO, IS THERE ANYONE HERE?"

Then she heard a faint voice from far, far, far away…

"We're down here!"

* * *

Dave was sitting in the waiting room of the hospital after his wife had gone into labour and the nurse walked out and said to the man sitting next to him, "Congratulations Ivan, you're the new father of twins!"

Ivan replied, "How about that! I work for Doublemint Chewing Gum!" He then followed the woman to his wife's room.

About an hour later, the same nurse entered the waiting room and announced that Mr Jones' wife had just had triplets. Mr Jones stood up and said, "Well, how do you like that! I work for 3M!"

Dave then got up and started to leave. The nurse asked him why he was leaving. "I think I need a breath of fresh air," Dave replied. "I work for 7-UP!"

* * *

Three expectant mothers were sitting in the obstetrician's waiting room. Two of the ladies began to chat about their pregnancies, and their due dates and so on.

The first woman said, "I happen to know that my baby is going to be a boy, because when my baby was conceived, my husband was on top."

The second replied, "Oh! That must mean that I'm going to have a girl, because when my baby was conceived, I was on top."

The third woman suddenly burst noisily into tears. Concerned, the other two ladies turned to her and asked, "My heavens, whatever is wrong?"

The woman wailed tearfully, "I'm having a puppy!"

* * *

As I got out of the car yesterday, my wife came running up to me in the drive, just jumping for joy! I didn't know why she was jumping for joy, but I thought "What the heck," and started jumping up and down with her.

She said, "Darling, I've got some great news for you!"

I said, "Great, tell me why you're so happy."

She stopped jumping and was breathing heavily from all the jumping up and down, when she told me she was pregnant! I was ecstatic because we had been trying for a while, so I grabbed her and kissed her on the lips and told her, "That's great – I couldn't be happier."

Then she said, "Oh, darling – there's more."

"What do you mean, more?" I asked.

"Well, we're not having one baby, we're going to have twins."

Amazed, I asked how she knew, and she replied, "That was the easy part, I went to the chemist and bought the twin-pack Home Pregnancy Test Kit, and both tests came out positive!"

* * *

A lonely frog telephones the Psychic Hotline and asks what his future holds. His Personal Psychic Advisor tells him, "You are going to meet a beautiful young girl who will want to know everything about you."

The frog is thrilled, "This is great! Will I meet her at a party?" he croaks.

"No," says the psychic. "In biology class."

* * *

John and Vicky were delighted when finally their long wait to adopt a baby came to an end. The adoption centre called and told them they had a wonderful Russian baby boy and the couple took him without hesitation.

On the way home from the adoption centre, they stopped by the local college so they each could enrol in night courses. After they filled out the form, the receptionist inquired, "What ever possessed you to study Russian?"

The couple said proudly, "We just adopted a Russian baby and in a year or so he'll start to talk. We just want to be able to understand him!"

Specialists

A dietician was once addressing a large audience in Chicago. "The material we put into our stomachs is enough to have killed most of us sitting here years ago. Red meat is awful. Soft drinks erode your stomach lining. Chinese food is loaded with MSG. Vegetables can be disastrous, and none of us realised the long-term harm caused by the germs in our drinking water.

"But there is one thing that is the most dangerous of all and we all have eaten it, or will eat it. Can anyone here tell me what food causes the longest-lasting grief and suffering after eating it?"

A 75-year-old man in the front row stood up and said, "Wedding cake."

* * *

Hello. Welcome to the Psychiatric Hotline.

- If you are obsessive-compulsive, please press 1 repeatedly.
- If you are co-dependent, please ask someone to press 2.
- If you have multiple personalities, please press 3, 4, 5, and 6.

- If you are paranoid-delusional, we know who you are and what you want. Just stay on the line so we can trace the call.
- If you are schizophrenic, listen carefully and a little voice will tell you which number to press.
- If you are manic-depressive, it doesn't matter which number you press. No one will answer.
- If you are anxious, just start pressing numbers at random.
- If you are phobic, don't press anything.
- If you are anal retentive, please hold.

* * *

Sarah had been feeling down for so long that she finally decided to seek the aid of a psychiatrist. She went there, lay on the couch, spilled her guts, then waited for the profound wisdom of the psychiatrist to make her feel better.

The psychiatrist asked her a few questions, took some notes, then sat thinking in silence for a few minutes with a puzzled look on his face. Suddenly, he looked up with an expression of delight and said, "Um, well, Sarah, I think your problem is low self-esteem. It's very common among losers."

* * *

Tom goes to a shrink and says, "Doctor, my wife is unfaithful to me. Every evening, she goes to John's bar and picks up men. In fact, she sleeps with anybody who asks her! I'm going crazy. What do you think I should do?"

"Relax," says the doctor, "take a deep breath and calm down. Now, tell me, exactly where is John's bar?"

* * *

I don't suffer from insanity. I enjoy every minute of it.

* * *

A Polish immigrant went to the DVLC to apply for a driver's license. First, they said he had to take an eye sight test. The optician showed him a card with letters: 'C Z W I X N O S T A C Z.'

"Can you read this?" the optician asked.

"Read it?" the Polish guy replied. "I know the guy."

* * *

John runs to the doctor and says, "Doctor, you've got to help me. Vicky thinks she's a chicken!"

The doctor asks, "How long has she had this condition?"

"Two years," says John.

"Then why did it take you so long to come and see me?" said the shrink.

John shrugs his shoulders and replies, "We needed the eggs."

* * *

A former radiologist tells that years ago, kitted up in leaden apron and gloves, he was conducting a radiographic examination of a woman's abdomen. Finding that her clothing was causing some opacity on the fluorescent screen, he remarked, "Would you pull down your knickers, please?" The patient did nothing, so he repeated the request. He then heard her say, "I'm so sorry, doctor. I thought you were talking to the nurse."

* * *

A gorgeous young redhead goes into the A and E and says that her body hurts wherever she touches it.

"Impossible!" says the doctor. "Show me."

The redhead takes her finger, pushes on her left breast and screams, then she pushes her elbow and screams in even more agony. She pushes her knee and screams; likewise she pushes her ankle and screams. Everywhere she touches makes her scream. The doctor says, "You're not really a redhead, are you?"

"Well, no," she says, "I'm actually a blonde."

"I thought so," the doctor says. "Your finger is broken!"

* * *

An agitated Jo was stomping around the psychiatrist's office, running her hands through her hair, almost in tears.

"Doctor, my memory's gone. Gone! I can't remember my husband's name. Can't remember my children's names. Can't remember what kind of car I drive. Can't remember where I work. It was all I could do to find my way here!"

"Calm down, Mrs Jones! How long have you been like this?"

"Like what?"

* * *

Norman and Edna were both patients in a mental hospital. One day while they were walking past the hospital swimming pool, Norman suddenly jumped into the deep end. He sank to the bottom of the pool and stayed there. Edna promptly jumped in to save him. She swam to the bottom and pulled Norman out.

When the Director heard of Edna's heroic act she immediately ordered her to be discharged from the hospital, considering her to be mentally stable.

She told Edna the news: "Edna, I have good news and bad news. The good news is you're being discharged. Since you were able to rationally respond to a crisis by jumping in and saving the life of another patient, I have concluded that your act displays soundness of mind. The bad news is that Norman hung himself right after you saved him with his dressing gown belt in the bathroom. I'm sorry, but he's dead."

Edna replied, "He didn't hang himself, I put him there to dry. How soon can I go home?"

* * *

Mrs Evans and her daughter were at the gynaecologist's office. The mother asked the doctor to examine her daughter. "She's been having some strange symptoms and I'm worried about her," the mother said.

The doctor examined the daughter and announced, "Mrs Evans, I believe your daughter is pregnant."

Mrs Evans gasped, "That's nonsense! Why, my little girl has nothing whatsoever to do with men." She turned to the girl. "You don't, do you, dear?"

"No, Mummy," said the girl. "Why, you know that I have never so much as kissed a man!"

The doctor looked from Mrs Evans to her daughter, and back again. Then, silently he stood up and walked to the window, staring out. He continued staring until Mrs Evans felt compelled to ask, "Doctor, is there something wrong out there?"

"No, Mrs Evans," said the doctor. "It's just that the last time anything like this happened, a star appeared in the East and I was looking to see if another one was going to show up."

* * *

A heart specialist doctor had died and it was his funeral. The coffin sat in front of a huge heart. When the pastor finished the sermon, and after everyone said their good-byes, the heart opened, the coffin rolled inside, and the heart closed. A beautiful way to go.

Just at that moment one of the mourners started laughing. The guy next to him asked, "Why are you laughing?"

"I was thinking about my own funeral," the man replied.

"What's so funny about that?"

"I'm a gynaecologist!"

* * *

Three elderly men are at the psychiatrist's surgery for a memory test. The psychiatrist asks the first man, "What is three times three?"

"274," is his reply. The psychiatrist rolls his eyes and looks up at the ceiling, and asks the second man, "It's your turn. What is three times three?"

"Tuesday," replies the second man. The psychiatrist shakes his head sadly, then asks the third man, "Okay, your turn. What's three times three?"

"Nine," says the third man.

"That's great!" says the psychiatrist. "How did you get that?"

"Simple," he says, "just subtract 274 from Tuesday."

* * *

Some friends were playing a round of golf when they heard shouts in the distance. Looking across, they watched in amazement as a buxom lady ran onto the fairway, pulled off some of her clothes and sprinted off up the course. Not two minutes later, two men in white coats appeared and asked which way the woman had gone. They pointed up the course and the two men ran off in that direction.

Bemused, the golfers carried on with their game, but were again disturbed, this time by a man staggering over the hill, panting with the effort of carrying two buckets of sand. Between wheezes, the newcomer asked which way the woman had gone, and then tottered away.

Increasingly baffled, the golf party ran after the figure. "What the hell is going on?" they asked. Gasping, the man explained: "The lady has escaped from our treatment clinic. She has acute nymphomania, and as soon as she gets all her clothes off, the nearest man is ravished."

"But why do you need two buckets of sand?" shouted the golfers after him.

"Well, I caught her the last time she escaped," panted the man. "This time, I needed a handicap."

* * *

A man who thought he was John the Baptist was disturbing the neighbourhood, so as a matter of public safety, he was committed. He was put in a room with another crazy man, and immediately began his routine, "I am John The Baptist! Jesus Christ sent me!"

The other guy looked at him and declared, "I did not!"

* * *

What do you get if you cross an agnostic, an insomniac and a dyslexic?

A man who lies awake at night, wondering if there really is a dog.

* * *

Doctors have developed a new pill that will now help impotent men who are also hay fever sufferers. By combining Allegra to take care of allergies, and Viagra for impotency, it gives you an erection not to be sneezed at!

* * *

The head doctors in a lunatic asylum had a meeting and decided that one of their patients was potentially well. So they decided to test him, and took him to see a film.

When they got to the cinema, there were 'wet paint' signs pointing to the benches. The doctors just sat down, but the patient put a newspaper down first before sitting down. The doctors got all excited, thinking he might be in touch with reality now. So they asked him, "Why did you put the newspaper down first?"

He replied, "So I'd be higher and have a better view!"

* * *

Three woman and their children were outside their psychiatrist's office. The wily old doctor was able to diagnose any complaint after asking the patient a few questions. The first woman went in and the doctor asked her a few questions and proclaimed: "Madam, all you ever think of is food. That is why you named your daughter Candy."

"Why," exclaimed the woman, "you're absolutely right, doctor!"

Then it was the second woman's turn. She got the same treatment and the doctor pronounced: "Madam, you're obsessed with the thought of money. That is why you named you daughter Penny."

"You're right, doctor!" exclaimed the second woman and left.

The third woman, who had been listening to all this, got up indignantly and said, "What rubbish! I don't believe a single word you said. Obsessions indeed!"

Then waving to her little son to follow her, she said, "Let's go home now, Dick."

* * *

A man goes to a psychiatrist. To start things off, the psychiatrist suggests they start with a Rorschach test. He holds up the first picture and asks the man what he sees. "A man and a woman making love in a park," the man replies.

The psychiatrist holds up the second picture and asks the man what he sees. "A man and a woman making love in a boat."

He holds up the third picture. "A man and a woman making love at the beach." This goes on for the rest of the set of pictures; the man says he sees a man and a woman making love in every one of the pictures.

At the end of the test, the psychiatrist looks over his notes and says, "It looks like you have a preoccupation with sex."

And the man replies, "Well, you're the one with the dirty pictures."

* * *

Q: How do two psychiatrists greet each other?
A: You are fine. How am I?

Q: How many psychiatrists does it take to change a light bulb?
A: Only one, but the light bulb has to WANT to change.

Q: How do crazy people go through the forest?
A: They take the psycho path.

* * *

Dr Llywellyn, the head psychiatrist at the local mental hospital, is examining patients to see if they're cured and ready to re-enter society.

"So, Mr Clark," the doctor says to one of his patients, "I see from your chart that you're recommended for dismissal. Do you have any idea what you might do once you're released?"

The patient thinks for a moment, then replies, "Well, I studied mechanical engineering. That's still a good field, so I could make some good money there. But on the other hand, I thought I might write a book about my experience here in the hospital, explaining what it's like to be a patient here. People might be interested in reading a book like that. In addition, I thought I might go back to college and study art history, which I've grown interested in lately."

Dr Llywellyn nods and says, "Yes, those all sound like intriguing possibilities."

The patient replies, "And the best part is, in my spare time, I can continue being a teapot!"

* * *

Aspiring student psychiatrists from various colleges were attending their first class on emotional extremes.

"Just to establish some parameters," said the professor to the first student, "what is the opposite of joy?"

"Sadness," replied the student.

"And the opposite of depression?" the professor asked of the second.

"Elation," said she.

"And you, sir," he said to the third. "How about the opposite of woe?"

The young lad replied, "I believe that would be giddy-up."

* * *

Evan walked into the hospital reception and the receptionist says, "Can I help you sir?"

He replied, "I've got shingles." She said, "Fill out this form and supply your name, address, and medical insurance number. When you're done, please take a seat." Fifteen minutes later a nurse's aide came out and asked him what he had.

He said, "Shingles." So she took down his height, weight, and complete medical history, then said, "Change into this gown and wait in the examining room."

Half an hour later a nurse came in and asked him what he had. He said, "Shingles." So she gave him a blood test, a blood pressure test, an electrocardiogram, and told him to wait for the doctor.

An hour later the doctor came in and asked him what he had. He said, "Shingles." The doctor gave him a full-cavity examination, and then said, "I just checked you out thoroughly, and I can't find shingles anywhere." Evan replied, "They're outside in the truck. Where do you want them?"

The Elderly

At a nursing home, a group of senior citizens were sitting around talking about their aches and pains.

"My arms are so weak I can hardly lift this cup of coffee," said one.

"I can't turn my head because of the arthritis in my neck," said a second.

"My blood pressure pills make me dizzy," another contributed.

"I guess that's the price we pay for getting old," winked an old man.

Then there was a short moment of silence.

"Thank god we can all still drive," said one woman cheerfully.

* * *

Two elderly residents, a man and a woman, were sitting alone in the lobby of their nursing home one evening. John looked over and said to Vicky, "I know just what you're wanting, for £5 I'll have sex with you right over there in that rocking chair."

Vicky looked surprised but didn't say a word. John continued, "For £10 I'll do it with you on that nice soft sofa over there, but for £20 I'll take you back to my room, light some candles, and give you the most romantic evening you've ever had in your life." Vicky still says nothing but after a couple of minutes, starts digging down in her purse. She pulls out a wrinkled £20 note and holds it up.

"So… you want the nice romantic evening in my room," says John.

"Get serious," she replies. "Four times in the rocking chair."

* * *

An old couple go to a doctor and ask him to watch them have sex and tell them if he sees them doing anything wrong. So they have sex. While they're getting dressed the doctor said, "I don't see anything wrong."

A week later they come again and ask the doctor to watch to see if they are doing anything wrong. They have sex and the doctor says, "Again, I don't see anything wrong."

This goes on for weeks. Then the doctor asks why they keep coming.

John says, "If we go to Vicky's house her husband will catch us. If we go to my house my wife will catch us. A hotel costs £50. Here it's £35 and p.p.p. pays half!"

* * *

"How did it happen?" the doctor asked Bob, a middle-aged farmhand, as he set the man's broken leg.

"Well, doc, 25 years ago…"

"Never mind the past. Tell me how you broke your leg this morning."

"Like I was saying… 25 years ago, when I first started working on the farm, that night, right after I'd gone to bed, the farmer's beautiful daughter came into my room. She asked me if there was anything I wanted. I said, 'No, everything's fine.'

'Are you sure?' she asked.

'I'm sure,' I said.

'Isn't there anything I can do for you?' she wanted to know.

'I reckon not,' I replied."

"Excuse me," said the doctor, "What does this story have to do with your leg?"

"Well, this morning," Bob explained, "when it dawned on me what she meant, I fell off the roof!"

* * *

An old couple go to the doctor. David goes first to have his physical. When the doctor is done with him, he sends the him back into the waiting room and calls Sue in. The doctor tells her, "Before we proceed with the examination, I would like to talk to you about David first."

Sue says, "Oh, no, it's his heart! I told him to lay

off the eggs."

The doctor says, "Well, I asked David how he was feeling, and he told me he felt great. He said that when he got up to go to the bathroom, he opened the door and God turned the light on for him. When he was done, he would shut the door, and God would turn the light out for him."

Sue replied, "Damn it, he's peeing in the fridge again!"

* * *

An 80-year-old couple were having problems remembering things, so they decided to go to their doctor to get checked out to make sure nothing was wrong with them. When they arrived at the doctor's, they explained to the doctor about the problems they were having with their memories. After checking the couple out, the doctor told them that they were physically okay, but might want to start writing things down and making notes to help them remember things. The couple thanked the doctor and left.

Later that night while watching television, the man got up from his chair and his wife asked, "Where are you going?"

He replied, "To the kitchen."

She asked, "Will you get me a bowl of ice cream?"

He replied, "Of course."

She then asked him, "Don't you think you should

write it down so you can remember it?"

He said, "No, I can remember that."

She then said, "Well, I'd also like some strawberries on top. You'd better write that down, because I know you'll forget that."

He said, "I can remember that! You want a bowl of ice cream with strawberries."

She replied, "I'd also would like whipped cream on top. I know you'll forget that, so you'd better write it down."

Irritated, he said, "I don't need to write that down! I can remember that." He then fumes into the kitchen. After about 20 minutes he returned from the kitchen and handed her a plate of bacon and eggs.

She stared at the plate for a moment, and said angrily, "I TOLD you to write it down! You forgot my toast!"

* * *

Two old men, reminiscing about the old times:

"Do you know, Sid, when I was just a lad, I never slept with my wife before we got married. Did you?"

"I don't know," said Alf. "What was her maiden name?"

* * *

Three old men are talking about their aches, pains and bodily functions.

The 70-year-old man says, "I have this problem. I wake up every morning at seven and it takes me 20 minutes to pee."

The 80-year-old man says, "My case is worse. I get up at eight and I sit there and grunt and groan for half an hour before I finally have a bowel movement."

The 90-year-old man says, "At seven I pee like a horse, and at eight I crap like a cow."

"So what's your problem?" ask the others.

"I don't wake up until nine!"

* * *

"You're in remarkable shape for a man your age," said the doctor to the 90-year-old man after the examination.

"I know it," said the old gentleman. "I've really got only one complaint – my sex drive is too high. Is there anything you can do for that?"

The doctor's mouth dropped open. "Your what?!" he gasped.

"My sex drive," said the old man. "It's too high, and I'd like you to lower it, if you can."

"Lower it?!" exclaimed the doctor, still unable to believe what the 90-year-old gent was saying. "Just what do you consider 'high'?"

"These days it seems like it's all in my head, Doc," said the old man, "and I'd like to have you lower it a couple of feet if you can."

* * *

A retired professor visits his doctor for a routine check-up, and everything seems fine. The doctor asks him about his sex life.

"Well…" the professor drawled, "not bad at all, to be honest. The wife isn't all that interested any more, so I just cruise around. In the past week I was able to pick up and bed at least three girls, none of whom were over 30 years old."

"My goodness! And at your age too," the doctor said. "I hope you at least took some precautions."

"Yep. I may be old, but I'm not senile yet, doc. I gave them all a false name!"

* * *

Bethany passed away and Bob called for an ambulance. The operator told Bob that she would send someone out right away.

"Where do you live?" asked the operator.

Bob replied, "At the end of Chalybeate Street."

The operator asked, "Can you spell that for me?"

There was a long pause and finally Bob said, "How about if I drag her over to Oak Street and you pick her up there?"

* * *

A woman was admitted for surgery. On the day of her surgery, she had a near-death experience but was fortunately resuscitated. After awakening in the ICU she told her nurses and doctors that she was so happy to be alive, and that she would fear death no longer. When asked why, she replied, "God told me it wasn't my time, so I don't have to worry about anything. He said I still have a long life to live."

When the women was released she would later return to the hospital on numerous occasions, always telling her nurses and doctors not to worry because of what God had told her. On each visit to the hospital, she would have plastic surgery in order to maintain her look of youth.

One day, to the surprise of both her nurses and doctors, she was rushed to the emergency room after being hit by a car. The woman, now looking great after her numerous plastic surgery operations, had died. This amazed both doctors and nurses. When the woman finally saw the golden gates and saw God she asked, "Why am I dead? You told me I still had a long life to live."

God replied, "Oops, it isn't your time! But I didn't recognize you!"

* * *

Harry is on his death bed, his wife Zelda is by his side.

"Zelda, you've always been by my side. When I broke my leg at 25, you were by my side. When I had my first heart attack at 45, you were by my side.

When I had my second heart attack at 65, you were by my side. When I broke my hip at 75, you were by my side. And now when I'm dying, you are at my side. Zelda, you're a bloody jinx!!"

* * *

The old couple went to Benidorm for their two-week holiday, but alas, the day before they were due to return, Jack collapsed and died.

As friends and relatives filed past his coffin at the funeral, Rose turned to the widow and remarked, "Gosh, Ethel, he looks wonderful."

"Oh yes," agreed Ethel, "Those two weeks in Benidorm did him the world of good!"

* * *

How about the two old men, one a retired professor of psychology and the other a retired professor of history. Their wives had talked them into a two-week stay at a hotel in the Cardiff Bay. They were sitting around on the porch of the hotel watching the sun set. The history professor said to the psychology professor, "Have you read Marx?"

To which the professor of psychology said, "Yes, I think it's the wicker chairs."

* * *

Ivan goes to the doctor and gets a check-up. The doctor finishes the exam and tells Ivan, "I have some bad news for you. You only have about two weeks left to live."

Ivan, obviously shocked, asks the doctor, "Is there is anything you can do to make the time that I have left more tolerable?"

The doctor thinks for a moment. "There is one thing that you could do."

"Just name it, I'll do whatever it is."

He tells Ivan to take a lot of mud baths, two or three a day.

Ivan looks at his doctor asks, "Will that help my condition?"

The doctor says, "No, but it will get you used to the dirt."

* * *

Sue was on her deathbed with husband, Jack, maintaining a steady vigil by her side. His warm tears splashed upon her face and woke her from her near-death slumber. "Jack darling," she whispered.

"Hush, my love," he said.

But she was insistent. "I need to confess something to you."

"There's nothing to confess. Don't worry yourself," Jack said tenderly.

"No, no – I must die in peace. I have been unfaithful to you with your father, your brother and your best friend," she croaked pathetically.

"Hush now, Sue – don't torment yourself, I know all about it," he said. "Why do you think I poisoned you?"

* * *

Brenda is at home making dinner as usual, when Tom arrives at her door.

"Brenda, can I come in?" he asks. "I've somethin' to tell you."

"Of course you can come in, you're always welcome, Tom. But where's my Ian?"

"That's what I'm here to tell you, Brenda. There was an accident down at the brewery…"

"Oh, God no!" cries Brenda. "Please don't tell me."

"I must, Brenda. Your husband Ian is dead and gone. I'm sorry."

Finally, she looked up at Tom.

"How did it happen, Tom?"

"It was terrible, Brenda. He fell into a vat of ale and drowned."

"Oh dear me! But you must tell me true, Tom. Did my Ian at least go quickly?"

"Well, Brenda… no. In fact, he got out three times to pee."

* * *

Vicky, on her deathbed, called her husband John and instructed him to look under their bed and open the wooden box he found. He was puzzled by the three eggs and £4,000 in cash he found in the box, so he asked his wife what the eggs were for.

"Oh those," she replied, "every time we had bad sex, I put an egg in the box."

Not bad, the husband thought to himself, after 35 years of marriage. Then he asked, "But what about the £4,000?"

"Oh that," she replied, "every time I got a dozen I sold them."

* * *

Living Will Form

I, _____, being of sound mind and body, do not wish to be kept alive indefinitely by artificial means.

Under no circumstances should my fate be put in the hands of pinhead politicians who couldn't pass ninth-grade biology if their lives depended on it. Nor in the hands of lawyers/doctors who are interested simply in running up the bills.

If a reasonable amount of time passes and I fail to ask for at least one of the following:

Bloody Mary,
Margarita,
Scotch and soda,
Martini,
Vodka and Tonic,

steak,
lobster or crab legs,
the remote control,
bowl of ice cream,
the sports page,
chocolate,
or sex
… it should be presumed that I won't ever get
better.

When such a determination is reached, I hereby
instruct my appointed person and attending
physicians to pull the plug, reel in the tubes and call it
a day.

At this point, it is time to call a New Orleans Jazz
Funeral Band to come do their thing at my funeral,
and ask all of my friends to raise their glasses to toast
the good times we have had.

Signature: _____

Date: _____

I also hear that in Ireland they have a Nursing
Home with a Pub. The patients are happier and they
have a lot more visitors.

D.H.S.S.

Having recently retired, David went to the D.H.S.S. office to apply for his pension.

The assistant behind the counter asked him for his driver's license to verify his age. He looked in his pockets and realized he had left his wallet at home. David told the woman that he was very sorry but he seemed to have left his wallet at home. "I'll have to go home and come back later," he said.

The assistant says, "Unbutton your shirt." So David opens his shirt revealing curly silver hair. She says, "David, that silver hair on your chest is proof enough for me," and she processed his pension application.

When he returned home, David excitedly tells his wife Vicky about his experience at the D.H.S.S. office.

She says, "You should have dropped your pants. You might have got the disability pension too."

* * *

The following are all replies that women have put on British Child Support Agency forms in the section for listing father's details:

1. Regarding the identity of the father of my twins, child A was fathered by [name removed]. I am unsure as to the identity of the father of child B, but I believe that he was conceived on the same night.

2. I am unsure as to the identity of the father of my child as I was being sick out of a window when taken unexpectedly from behind. I can provide you with a list of names of men that I think were at the party if this helps.

3. I do not know the name of the father of my little girl. She was conceived at a party [address and date given] where I had unprotected sex with a man I met that night. I do remember that the sex was so good that I fainted. If you do manage to track down the father can you send me his phone number? Thanks.

4. I don't know the identity of the father of my daughter. He drives a BMW that now has a hole made by my stiletto in one of the door panels. Perhaps you can contact BMW service stations in this area and see if he's had it replaced.

5. I have never had sex with a man. I am awaiting a letter from the Pope confirming that my son's conception was immaculate and that he is Christ risen again.

6. I cannot tell you the name of child A's dad as he

informs me that to do so would blow his cover and that would have cataclysmic implications for the British economy. I am torn between doing right by you and right by the country. Please advise.

7. I do not know who the father of my child was, as all squaddies look the same to me. I can confirm that he was a Royal Green Jacket.

8. [name given] is the father of child A. If you do catch up with him can you ask him what he did with my AC/DC CDs?

9. From the dates it seems that my daughter was conceived at Euro Disney. Maybe it really is the Magic Kingdom.

10. So much about that night is a blur. The only thing that I remember for sure is Delia Smith did a programme about eggs earlier in the evening. If I'd stayed in and watched more TV rather than going to the party at [address given] mine might have remained unfertilised.

Viagra Jokes

Scotland Yard are having a crackdown on Viagra smugglers. Police are reported to be looking for 20 hardened criminals.

* * *

John, who was at a nursing home, took Viagra and went to the dining room, where all the residents were playing Bingo. To get their attention he yelled out, "Super Sex! Super Sex!"

The ladies yelled back, "Soup, Please!"

* * *

There are some new Viagra eye drops on the market. They make you look hard.

* * *

John spent too much money on Viagra: now he's hard up.

* * *

Did you hear about the first death caused from an overdose of Viagra? John took twelve pills and his wife died.

* * *

Dave went to the pharmacy to pick up his Viagra prescription and complained over the £6 pill price. Megan, who was with him, had a different opinion: "Oh, £6 a year isn't too bad."

* * *

…Then there was John who got his Viagra tablet stuck in his throat and suffered from a stiff neck.

* * *

If you're depressed and think you might need Viagra, see a professional. If that doesn't work, see a doctor!

* * *

Bob left his Viagra tablet in his shirt pocket when he sent it to the laundry. Now, his shirt is too stiff to wear.

* * *

It is no longer necessary to stake tomatoes. Just dissolve a Viagra tablet in the water and they stand up straight and tall.

* * *

Viagra is now being compared to Disneyland – a one-hour wait for a 2-minute ride.

* * *

Men taking iron supplements are warned that taking Viagra may cause them to spin around and point north.

* * *

Rumour has it that when a lorry carrying a load of Viagra slid off into the River Thames, the Tower bridge suddenly went up.

* * *

For years the medical professional has been looking after the ill, to make them better. Now, with Viagra, they're raising the dead!

* * *

The difference between Niagara and Viagra?
Niagara Falls.

* * *

Unconfirmed but frequent reports tell us that a man who overdosed on Viagra caused the funeral home problems – they couldn't close his coffin lid for three days.

* * *

Viagra has been a big boon to stand-up comedians.

* * *

A Viagra delivery truck was hijacked on the M4. The police are looking for hardened criminals. They can expect a stiff penalty.

* * *

Ivan goes to visit his 85-year-old grandfather in the hospital.

"How are you?" he asks.

"Feeling fine," says the old chap.

"What's the food like?"

"Terrific, wonderful menus."

"And the nursing?"

"Just couldn't be better. These young nurses really take care of you."

"What about sleeping? Do you sleep OK?"

"No problem at all… nine hours solid every night. At 10 o'clock they bring me a cup of hot chocolate and a Viagra tablet… and that's it. I go out like a light."

Ivan is puzzled and a little alarmed by this, so rushes off to question the Sister in charge.

"What are you people doing?" he says, "my granddad told me you're giving him, an 85-year-old, Viagra on a daily basis. Surely that can't be true?"

"Oh, yes," replies the Sister. "Every night at 10 o'clock we give him a cup of hot chocolate and a Viagra tablet. It works wonderfully well. The hot chocolate makes him sleep, and the Viagra stops him from rolling out of bed."

Hospital Jokes is just one of a whole
range of publications from Y Lolfa.
For a full list of books currently in print,
send now for your free copy
of our new full-colour catalogue.
Or simply surf into our website

www.ylolfa.com

for secure on-line ordering.

Talybont Ceredigion Cymru SY24 5AP
e-mail ylolfa@ylolfa.com
website www.ylolfa.com
phone (01970) 832 304
fax 832 782